Amazing Animals
Blue Whales

Angela Royston

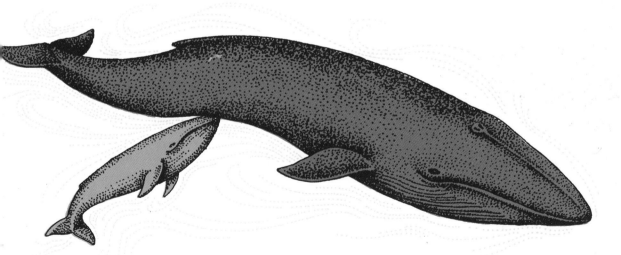

WEIGL PUBLISHERS INC.

Published by Weigl Publishers Inc.
350 5th Avenue, Suite 3304, PMB 6G
New York, NY 10114-0069

Amazing Animals series © 2010
WEIGL PUBLISHERS INC. www.weigl.com

Library of Congress Cataloging-in-
Publication Data available upon request.
Fax 1-866-44-WEIGL for the attention of
the Publishing Records department.

ISBN 978-1-60596-148-4 (hard cover)
ISBN 978-1-60596-149-1 (soft cover)

Editor
Heather Kissock
Design and Layout
Terry Paulhus, Kathryn Livingstone

Photograph Credits
Every reasonable effort has been
made to trace ownership and to obtain
permission to reprint copyright material.
The publishers would be pleased to have
any errors or omissions brought to their
attention so that they may be corrected
in subsequent printings.

Weigl acknowledges Getty Images as its
primary image supplier for this title.

Printed in China
1 2 3 4 5 6 7 8 9 0   13 12 11 10 09

About This Book

This book tells you all about blue whales. Find out where they live and what they eat. Discover how you can help to protect them. You can also read about them in myths and legends from around the world.

Words in **bold** are explained in the Words to Know section at the back of the book.

Useful Websites

Addresses in this book take you to the home pages of websites that have information about blue whales.

All of the Internet URLs given in the book were valid at the time of publication. However, due to the dynamic nature of the Internet, some addresses may have changed, or sites may have ceased to exist since publication. While the author and publisher regret any inconvenience this may cause readers, no responsibility for any such changes can be accepted by either the author or the publisher.

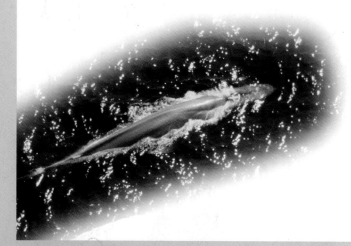

Contents

Meet the Blue Whale

Blue whales are gigantic animals that swim in the oceans. They are the largest animals on Earth. Whales may look like fish, but they are **mammals**. Like other mammals, they have hair on their bodies, and the mothers feed their babies with milk from their bodies.

▼ A blue whale has nostrils on top of its head for breathing in and out.

Whales cannot breathe underwater. They come to the surface of the ocean to take deep breaths of fresh air.

Useful Websites

www.whale-web.com

Learn all about the whale family by visiting this website.

The Whale Family

There are many different kinds of whales.

- blue whales
- dolphins
- gray whales
- humpback whales
- killer whales
- sperm whales

▲ A blue whale swims by moving its powerful tail up and down in the water.

A Very Special Animal

A whale's body is made for swimming and eating. Blue whales swim a long way to find food and to escape enemies.

A blue whale does not have teeth. Instead, it has tough, bristly strips in its mouth called **baleen plates**. These help the whale to catch and trap small ocean animals in its mouth.

▲ A blue whale's flippers help the animal steer through water.

The Amazing Blue Whale

- A blue whale's heart is as big as a small car.

- A blue whale weighs as much as 30 elephants.

- Blue whales can swim at 30 miles (48 kilometers) per hour. This is as fast as a car traveling in a town.

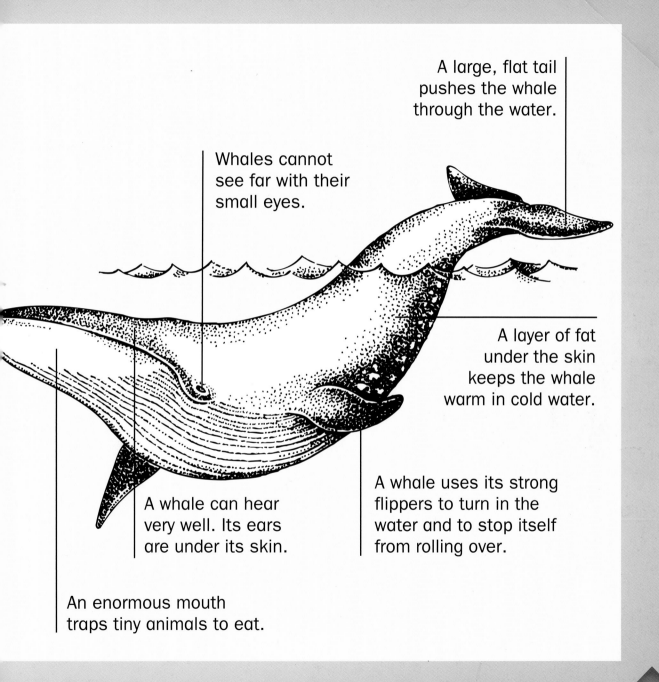

A large, flat tail pushes the whale through the water.

Whales cannot see far with their small eyes.

A layer of fat under the skin keeps the whale warm in cold water.

A whale can hear very well. Its ears are under its skin.

A whale uses its strong flippers to turn in the water and to stop itself from rolling over.

An enormous mouth traps tiny animals to eat.

How Whales Breathe

A blue whale breathes through nostrils called blowholes. The holes are on its back, near the head. When the whale needs to breathe in fresh air, it comes to the surface of the water. First it breathes out. A fine spray of water shoots high into the air. This spray is called a **spout**.

The whale breathes in and out a few times. Then, it holds its breath and dives below the surface again.

▶ A blue whale blows out a fine, misty spray through its blowholes.

Big Breaths

- A blue whale's spout can be as high as a four-story building.

- A blue whale can hold its breath for as long as one hour.

- You can hear a blue whale breathing from half a mile (800 meters) away.

▲ Blue whales often swim near the surface of the ocean so that they can come up for air easily.

How Blue Whales Eat

Blue whales feast on tiny, shrimp-like animals called **krill**. Millions of krill float near the surface of the ocean.

A blue whale takes in a large mouthful of krill and water. Then it closes its mouth and pushes the water out through its bristly baleen plates. The bristles trap the krill inside the whale's mouth. The whale then swallows its meal whole.

▶ Krill are about the size of a human thumb. A blue whale swallows thousands of krill each gulp.

A Big Appetite

- The amount of water in a swimming pool could fit inside a blue whale's mouth.

- Each day, a blue whale eats about four tons (3.6 tonnes) of food. A person would need to eat for two years to eat the same amount.

▲ A blue whale's mouth is one-quarter of the length of its body.

Where Whales Live

Blue whales live in all of the world's oceans. For most of the year, they live in the cold waters near the North and South Poles. Here they feed on krill. They store food as fat under their skin.

Blue whales swim to warmer waters to give birth to their **calves**. Food is hard to find in warm water. The whales stay for just a few months. Then, they swim back to the cold waters.

▼ Blue whales often return to the same place each year.

Useful Websites

www.tmmc.org

Read all about blue whales and other ocean animals on this website.

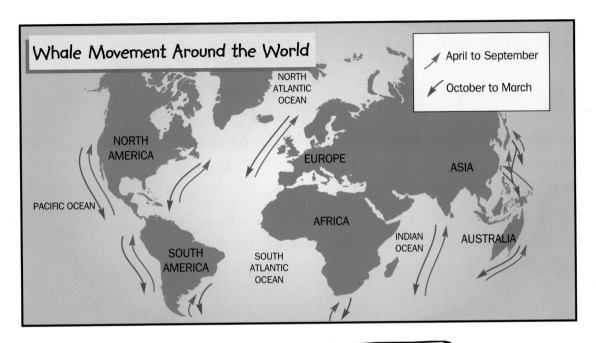

Whale Movement Around the World

April to September

October to March

NORTH ATLANTIC OCEAN

NORTH AMERICA

EUROPE

ASIA

PACIFIC OCEAN

AFRICA

INDIAN OCEAN

AUSTRALIA

SOUTH AMERICA

SOUTH ATLANTIC OCEAN

Blue Whale Companions

There are many different kinds of animals that spend time in the oceans with blue whales.

- dolphins and other whales
- krill and other tiny animals
- fish
- penguins
- seabirds
- seals
- shellfish
- squid

▲ Whales make long journeys through the oceans. This map shows where blue whales travel at different times of the year.

Friends and Enemies

Blue whales share their ocean home with penguins, seabirds, seals, and other whales. Now and then, whales may fight over food, but there is usually enough food for all. A blue whale's huge body provides a home for some small animals. **Barnacles** and **remora fish** attach themselves to the whale's skin.

▼ Killer whales have sharp teeth and hunt in groups.

Meat-eating killer whales are the only animals strong enough to attack a blue whale.

Useful Websites

www.enchantedlearning.com

Visit this website to find blue whale facts and activities.

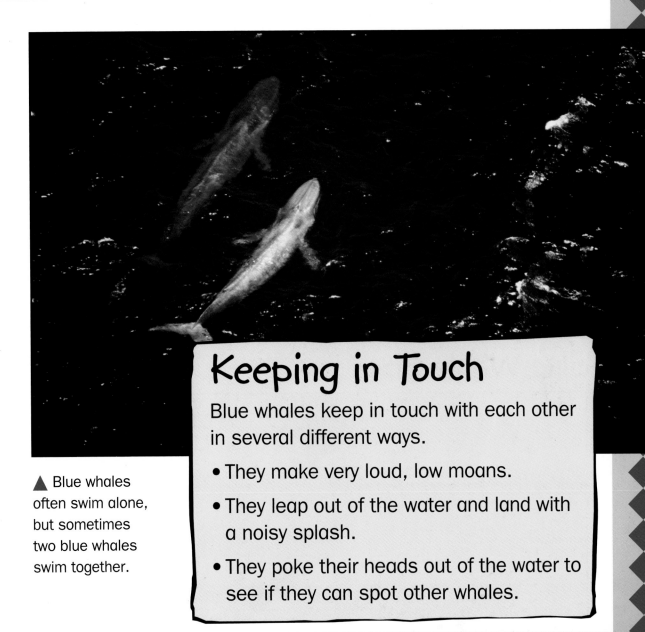

▲ Blue whales often swim alone, but sometimes two blue whales swim together.

Keeping in Touch

Blue whales keep in touch with each other in several different ways.

- They make very loud, low moans.
- They leap out of the water and land with a noisy splash.
- They poke their heads out of the water to see if they can spot other whales.

Growing Up

A mother blue whale gives birth to a calf under water. She quickly pushes the calf to the surface, where it takes its first breath of air.

A young calf is a good swimmer. It feeds on its mother's milk and follows her closely. When the calf is eight months old, it starts to find its own food and swim on its own.

Blue Whale Sizes

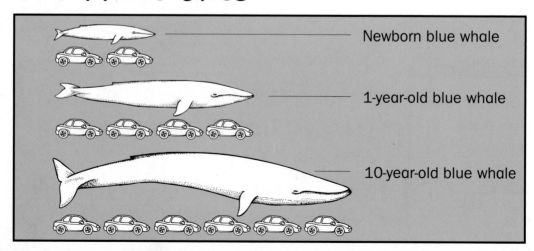

Newborn blue whale

1-year-old blue whale

10-year-old blue whale

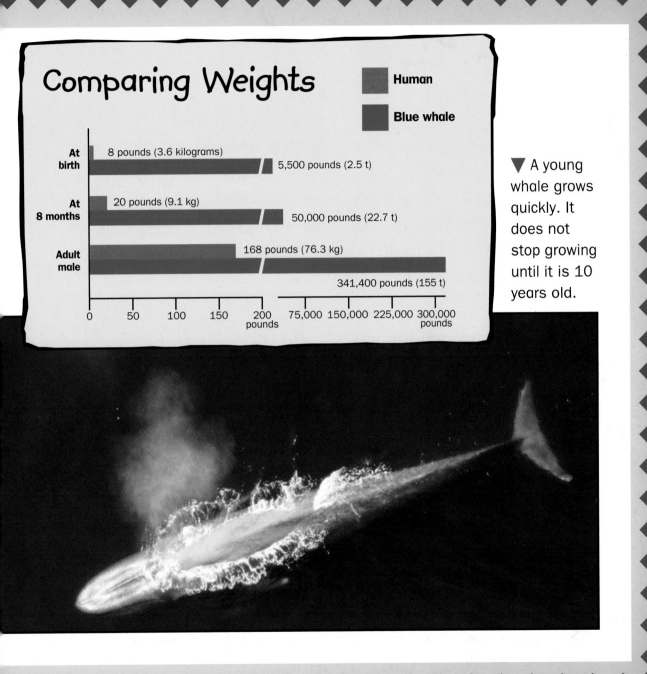

Comparing Weights

Human
Blue whale

At birth	8 pounds (3.6 kilograms)	5,500 pounds (2.5 t)
At 8 months	20 pounds (9.1 kg)	50,000 pounds (22.7 t)
Adult male	168 pounds (76.3 kg)	341,400 pounds (155 t)

| 0 | 50 | 100 | 150 | 200 pounds | 75,000 | 150,000 | 225,000 | 300,000 pounds |

▼ A young whale grows quickly. It does not stop growing until it is 10 years old.

Under Threat

For hundreds of years, people hunted whales. They killed so many in the past that some kinds of whales may soon die out altogether. In the 1970s, groups of people started trying to save the whales. Today, it is against the law to hunt blue whales.

▼ Whale-watching trips help people understand the blue whale and the threats it faces.

People still harm whales in other ways. Whales that swim near the coast sometimes swallow garbage. Whales also die when people spill oil and poisons into the sea.

Useful Websites

http://csiwhalesalive.org
www.whales-online.net

Visit these websites to find out how you can help protect whales.

▲ Many ocean animals are harmed by oil spills, including whales and birds.

What Do You Think?

Krill is the main food that blue whales eat. If people fish for krill, there might not be enough left for the whales. Should people be allowed to fish for krill? Or should people leave the krill for whales and other animals to eat?

Myths and Legends

For hundreds of years, people have told stories about whales.

▼ People used to think whales were giant sea monsters.

Sea Monsters

Sailors who saw whales told scary stories about them when they came home. For many years, people thought that whales were huge fish or monsters.

Swallowed by Whales

There are many stories about whales that swallow people and spit them out again.

- In the Bible, Jonah is swallowed by a whale. He lives in the whale's stomach for three days, then escapes unhurt.

- In the story of *Pinocchio*, a woodcarver and his son Pinocchio are swallowed by a fierce whale. They also escape.

Moby Dick

A writer named Herman Melville wrote a story about a whale named Moby Dick. The story features a sea captain who lost one of his legs in a fight with a whale. He searches the oceans for the whale so that he can fight it again.

▼ Moby Dick was a type of whale known as a sperm whale.

Quiz

1. What group of animals do whales belong to?
   (*a*) **mammals** (*b*) **reptiles** (*c*) **fish**

2. What do blue whales eat?
   (*a*) **seals** (*b*) **penguins** (*c*) **krill**

3. What are a whale's nostrils called?
   (*a*) **a blowhole** (*b*) **a baleen** (*c*) **a flipper**

4. Which animals may attack blue whales?
   (*a*) **seabirds** (*b*) **killer whales**
   (*c*) **dolphins**

5. What is a baby whale called?
   (*a*) **a pup** (*b*) **a calf** (*c*) **a cub**

Answers:
1. (a) Whales are mammals.
2. (c) Blue whales eat krill.
3. (a) A whale's nostrils are called a blowhole.
4. (b) Killer whales may attack blue whales.
5. (b) A baby whale is called a calf.

Find out More

To find out more about whales, visit the websites in this book. You can also write to these organizations.

Cetacean Society International
P.O. Box 9145
Wethersfield, CT 06109

Cousteau Society
930 West 21st Street
Norfolk, VA 23517

Whale and Dolphin Conservation Society
191 Weston Road
Lincoln, MA 01773

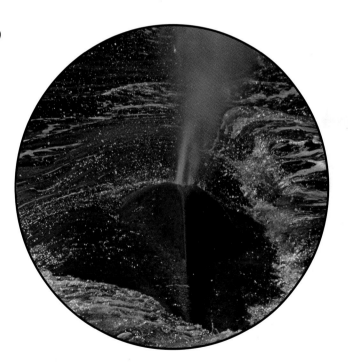

Words to Know

baleen plates
tough, bristly strips that trap food in a blue whale's mouth

barnacles
small shellfish that cling to rocks, ships, and some kinds of whales

calves
young or baby whales

krill
tiny, shrimp-like animals

mammals
animals that have hair or fur and feed milk to their young

remora fish
a fish that clings to other animals using a sucker on its head

spout
a fine spray of water that a whale makes when it breathes out

Index